EMMANUEL JOSEPH

Sovereign Shadows: The Dance of Nations

Copyright © 2025 by Emmanuel Joseph

All rights reserved. No part of this publication may be reproduced, stored or transmitted in any form or by any means, electronic, mechanical, photocopying, recording, scanning, or otherwise without written permission from the publisher. It is illegal to copy this book, post it to a website, or distribute it by any other means without permission.

First edition

This book was professionally typeset on Reedsy.
Find out more at reedsy.com

# Contents

| | | |
|---|---|---|
| 1 | Chapter 1: The Dawn of Sovereignty | 1 |
| 2 | Chapter 2: The Power of Diplomacy | 3 |
| 3 | Chapter 3: The Economics of Influence | 5 |
| 4 | Chapter 4: The Might of Military Power | 7 |
| 5 | Chapter 5: The Role of International Organizations | 9 |
| 6 | Chapter 6: Soft Power and Cultural Influence | 11 |
| 7 | Chapter 7: The Influence of Technology and Innovation | 13 |
| 8 | Chapter 8: Environmental Diplomacy and Global Challenges | 15 |
| 9 | Chapter 9: Human Rights and Moral Leadership | 17 |
| 10 | Chapter 10: Global Health and Pandemic Response | 19 |
| 11 | Chapter 11: The Influence of Media and Information | 21 |
| 12 | Chapter 12: The Interplay of Nationalism and Globalism | 23 |
| 13 | Chapter 13: The Influence of Religion and Ideology | 25 |
| 14 | Chapter 14: The Role of NonState Actors | 27 |
| 15 | Chapter 15: The Dynamics of Regionalism | 28 |
| 16 | Chapter 16: The Impact of Migration and Diasporas | 30 |
| 17 | Chapter 17: The Role of Intelligence and Espionage | 32 |
| 18 | Chapter 18: The Influence of Global Finance | 34 |
| 19 | Chapter 19: The Ethics of Sovereign Influence | 36 |
| 20 | Chapter 20: The Role of Science and Innovation in Global... | 38 |

# 1

# Chapter 1: The Dawn of Sovereignty

In the dawn of human civilization, the concept of sovereignty began to take root. Emerging from the primordial need for order and structure, early societies formed around strong leaders who could protect and guide their people. These leaders, often seen as divine or chosen by the gods, laid the foundations for what would become modern sovereign states. As time passed, the divine right of kings gave way to more secular and democratic forms of governance, but the fundamental principle of sovereignty remained.

Sovereignty is not just about power and control; it is about identity and autonomy. The sense of belonging to a sovereign state gives people a shared identity and a sense of purpose. It allows them to participate in a collective endeavor, striving for common goals and ideals. This sense of unity is crucial for the stability and prosperity of any nation.

However, sovereignty is also a doubleedged sword. While it can bring unity and strength, it can also lead to conflict and division. The desire for sovereignty has been the cause of countless wars and conflicts throughout history. The struggle for power and control over land and resources has led to the rise and fall of empires and the redrawing of borders. Even today, the quest for sovereignty continues to shape the political landscape of the world.

The concept of sovereignty is constantly evolving. In the modern era, the rise of globalization and interdependence has challenged traditional notions of sovereignty. Nationstates must navigate a complex web of international relations, balancing their own interests with those of other countries. This dance of nations requires diplomacy, negotiation, and sometimes, compromise.

As we delve deeper into the dance of nations, we will explore how sovereign states exert their influence on the global stage. From economic powerhouses to military might, from cultural influence to diplomatic prowess, the tools of statecraft are varied and powerful. In the chapters that follow, we will examine these tools in detail and explore how they are used to shape the world.

# 2

# Chapter 2: The Power of Diplomacy

Diplomacy is one of the oldest and most important tools of statecraft. It is the art of negotiation and communication between sovereign states. Through diplomacy, nations can resolve conflicts, build alliances, and promote their interests on the global stage. Diplomacy is often seen as a peaceful and constructive way to exert influence, but it can also be a tool of manipulation and coercion.

One of the key principles of diplomacy is mutual respect. Diplomatic negotiations are based on the recognition of the sovereignty and equality of all states. This principle is enshrined in international law and is the foundation of the United Nations. However, in practice, power imbalances and competing interests can complicate diplomatic efforts. Stronger states may use their influence to pressure weaker states into accepting unfavorable terms.

Diplomacy can take many forms, from formal negotiations and treaties to informal dialogues and backchannel communications. Diplomatic missions, embassies, and consulates play a crucial role in maintaining relations between states. Diplomats are skilled professionals who represent their country's interests and work to build and maintain positive relationships with other nations.

Economic diplomacy is a powerful tool that nations use to promote trade and investment. Through trade agreements, sanctions, and aid, countries can influence the economic behavior of other states. Economic powerhouses like the United States and China use their economic clout to shape global markets and advance their strategic interests.

Cultural diplomacy is another important aspect of statecraft. By promoting their culture and values abroad, nations can build soft power and enhance their global influence. Cultural exchange programs, international broadcasting, and public diplomacy efforts help to foster mutual understanding and goodwill between countries. In the age of globalization, cultural diplomacy has become an essential tool for building bridges between diverse societies.

Diplomacy is not without its challenges. In a world of competing interests and shifting alliances, diplomatic efforts can be undermined by mistrust, miscommunication, and conflicting agendas. However, the importance of diplomacy cannot be overstated. It is through diplomacy that nations can find common ground and work together to address global challenges, from climate change to terrorism.

# 3

# Chapter 3: The Economics of Influence

Economic power is a cornerstone of statecraft. Nations with strong economies can wield significant influence on the global stage. They can shape international markets, dictate trade terms, and provide aid and investment to other countries. Economic power is not just about wealth; it is about the ability to use that wealth to achieve strategic goals.

Trade is a key component of economic influence. By controlling access to markets and resources, nations can exert pressure on other states. Trade agreements and tariffs can be used to promote economic cooperation or to punish adversaries. The global nature of trade means that economic decisions in one country can have farreaching effects on the rest of the world.

Foreign aid is another tool of economic statecraft. By providing financial assistance to developing countries, donor nations can build alliances and promote their values. Aid can be used to support humanitarian efforts, foster economic development, and strengthen political stability. However, aid can also be a tool of manipulation, used to gain influence and control over recipient countries.

Investment is a powerful way for nations to extend their economic influence. By investing in infrastructure, industries, and technology in other countries, nations can build economic ties and promote mutual prosperity. Investment can create jobs, stimulate growth, and foster innovation. However, it can also lead to dependency and exploitation, as powerful nations seek to protect their investments and interests.

Economic sanctions are a form of coercive diplomacy. By imposing restrictions on trade and financial transactions, nations can pressure other states to change their behavior. Sanctions can be used to punish human rights abuses, prevent the proliferation of weapons, and address other international security concerns. However, sanctions can also have unintended consequences, harming innocent civilians and exacerbating economic hardships.

The global economy is interconnected, and economic decisions made by one nation can have ripple effects around the world. In the chapters that follow, we will explore how economic power shapes international relations and how nations use economic tools to achieve their strategic objectives.

# 4

# Chapter 4: The Might of Military Power

Military power is perhaps the most visible and immediate form of state influence. The ability to project force and defend sovereignty is a fundamental aspect of statecraft. Nations maintain armed forces not only to protect their own borders but also to exert influence and achieve strategic goals on the global stage.

Throughout history, military power has been used to conquer territories, deter adversaries, and maintain order. The threat of military force can be a powerful deterrent, preventing conflicts and maintaining stability. However, the use of force can also lead to destruction, loss of life, and longterm instability.

Modern military power is not just about sheer numbers and firepower. It is also about technology, intelligence, and strategy. Advanced weaponry, surveillance systems, and cyber capabilities are essential components of contemporary military strength. Nations invest heavily in research and development to maintain a technological edge over potential adversaries.

Alliances and military partnerships play a crucial role in enhancing a nation's military influence. Through alliances like NATO, countries can pool their resources and coordinate their defense efforts. These partnerships can serve as a deterrent to potential aggressors and promote collective security.

Peacekeeping and humanitarian missions are important aspects of modern military operations. Nations deploy their armed forces to conflict zones and disaster areas to restore peace, provide aid, and support reconstruction efforts. These missions demonstrate a nation's commitment to global stability and humanitarian values.

However, the use of military power is not without controversy. Military interventions can be perceived as acts of aggression and can lead to longterm resentment and instability. The ethical and legal implications of using force are complex and often debated. In the chapters that follow, we will examine the role of military power in international relations and explore the balance between force and diplomacy.

# 5

# Chapter 5: The Role of International Organizations

International organizations play a pivotal role in the dance of nations. These institutions provide a platform for cooperation, dialogue, and collective action. They help to address global challenges, promote peace and security, and facilitate economic development. The United Nations, the World Bank, the International Monetary Fund, and the World Trade Organization are just a few examples of key international organizations.

The United Nations (UN) is perhaps the most wellknown international organization. Established in 1945, the UN aims to promote peace, security, and human rights. It provides a forum for member states to discuss and resolve conflicts, coordinate humanitarian efforts, and address global issues like climate change and poverty. The Security Council, General Assembly, and various specialized agencies play crucial roles in the UN's work.

The World Bank and the International Monetary Fund (IMF) are key players in the global economy. The World Bank provides financial and technical assistance to developing countries, supporting projects that promote economic development and reduce poverty. The IMF, on the other hand, aims to ensure the stability of the international monetary system by providing financial support and policy advice to member states facing economic challenges.

The World Trade Organization (WTO) oversees international trade rules and promotes free and fair trade. It provides a platform for member states to negotiate trade agreements and resolve disputes. The WTO aims to create a level playing field for all countries, promoting economic growth and development through trade.

Regional organizations also play a significant role in international relations. The European Union (EU), the African Union (AU), the Association of Southeast Asian Nations (ASEAN), and the Organization of American States (OAS) are just a few examples. These organizations promote regional integration, cooperation, and development. They provide a forum for member states to address common challenges and pursue shared goals.

International organizations face numerous challenges. They must navigate the competing interests and agendas of member states, address limited resources and capacities, and adapt to an everchanging global landscape. However, their role in promoting cooperation, peace, and development cannot be overstated.

# 6

# Chapter 6: Soft Power and Cultural Influence

Soft power is the ability to attract and coopt rather than coerce. It is the subtle and indirect way in which nations exert influence through cultural appeal, values, and foreign policy. Unlike hard power, which relies on military and economic might, soft power is about winning hearts and minds.

Cultural influence is a major component of soft power. Through music, movies, literature, and art, nations can project their culture and values to a global audience. Hollywood movies, Kpop music, and French cuisine are examples of cultural exports that have won global admiration. These cultural products create a positive image of their countries of origin and foster goodwill.

Educational exchanges and scholarships are another way nations build soft power. By welcoming international students and offering scholarships, countries can build lasting relationships and influence future leaders. These exchanges promote mutual understanding and create networks of alumni who have a positive view of the host country.

Public diplomacy and international broadcasting are essential tools of soft power. Nations use media to communicate their values and policies to a global audience. Television networks like the BBC, Al Jazeera, and CNN have a worldwide reach and can shape public opinion. Social media has also become a powerful tool for public diplomacy, allowing nations to engage directly with people around the world.

Soft power is not just about culture and communication; it is also about demonstrating moral leadership. Nations that uphold human rights, support humanitarian efforts, and promote peace can build a positive reputation. This moral authority can be a powerful source of influence.

However, soft power is not without its limitations. It can be difficult to measure and its effects may take time to manifest. Additionally, soft power can be undermined by negative actions or policies that contradict the values a nation seeks to promote. Despite these challenges, soft power remains a crucial aspect of statecraft in the modern world.

# 7

# Chapter 7: The Influence of Technology and Innovation

Technology and innovation are driving forces in the dance of nations. Advances in technology can reshape economies, alter the balance of power, and create new opportunities for cooperation and competition. Nations that lead in technology and innovation have a significant advantage on the global stage.

The digital revolution has transformed the way nations interact. The internet and social media have created new platforms for communication and influence. Cybersecurity has become a critical aspect of national security, as nations seek to protect their digital infrastructure and information.

Innovation in science and technology can drive economic growth and enhance a nation's competitiveness. Countries that invest in research and development can lead in fields like artificial intelligence, biotechnology, and renewable energy. These technological advancements can create new industries, jobs, and economic opportunities.

Space exploration is another frontier of technological competition and cooperation. Nations invest in space programs to enhance their technological capabilities and assert their presence in space. International collaboration on space missions can promote scientific progress and build trust between nations.

Technology also plays a key role in addressing global challenges. Innovations in healthcare, agriculture, and energy can improve the quality of life for people around the world. Nations that lead in these areas can contribute to global development and enhance their soft power.

However, technological competition can also lead to tensions and conflicts. Intellectual property disputes, cyber attacks, and competition for resources can create friction between nations. Balancing cooperation and competition in the realm of technology is a complex challenge for statecraft.

# 8

# Chapter 8: Environmental Diplomacy and Global Challenges

Environmental issues are among the most pressing challenges facing the world today. Climate change, pollution, and resource depletion have farreaching consequences for all nations. Environmental diplomacy is the effort to address these challenges through international cooperation and agreements.

Climate change is a global problem that requires a collective response. International agreements like the Paris Agreement aim to limit global warming and reduce greenhouse gas emissions. Nations work together to set targets, share technologies, and provide financial support for climate action.

Conservation and biodiversity are also important aspects of environmental diplomacy. Protecting natural habitats, endangered species, and marine ecosystems requires coordinated efforts. International conventions like the Convention on Biological Diversity and the Ramsar Convention on Wetlands promote conservation and sustainable use of natural resources.

Resource management is a critical issue for environmental diplomacy. Access to clean water, arable land, and energy resources is essential for sustainable development. Nations must cooperate to manage shared resources and prevent conflicts over scarcity.

Disaster response and resilience are important components of environmental diplomacy. Natural disasters like hurricanes, earthquakes, and floods can have devastating impacts. International cooperation on disaster preparedness, response, and recovery can save lives and reduce suffering.

Environmental diplomacy faces significant challenges. Differing priorities, economic interests, and political will can hinder progress. However, the urgency of environmental issues makes cooperation essential. Through environmental diplomacy, nations can work together to protect the planet and ensure a sustainable future for all.

# 9

# Chapter 9: Human Rights and Moral Leadership

Human rights are a cornerstone of international relations and diplomacy. The promotion and protection of human rights are fundamental principles enshrined in international law and institutions. Nations that uphold human rights can build moral authority and influence on the global stage.

The Universal Declaration of Human Rights, adopted by the United Nations in 1948, sets out fundamental rights and freedoms for all people. These rights include the right to life, liberty, and security, as well as freedom of expression, assembly, and religion. International human rights treaties and conventions further elaborate on these rights and establish mechanisms for their protection.

Nations promote human rights through diplomatic efforts, advocacy, and support for international institutions. Diplomats engage in dialogue, negotiations, and public statements to address human rights concerns. Countries may also provide support for human rights organizations, activists, and defenders.

Humanitarian aid and intervention are important aspects of promoting human rights. Nations provide assistance to people affected by conflicts, natural disasters, and human rights abuses. Humanitarian aid can include food, medical care, shelter, and education. In some cases, military intervention may be necessary to protect civilians and prevent atrocities.

The promotion of human rights is not without challenges. Human rights violations persist in many parts of the world, and efforts to address them can be complicated by political, economic, and cultural factors. Nations may face criticism for their own human rights records, and balancing national interests with moral imperatives can be difficult.

Despite these challenges, the promotion of human rights is essential for building a just and peaceful world. Nations that lead in this area can build moral authority and influence, contributing to global stability and prosperity.

# 10

# Chapter 10: Global Health and Pandemic Response

Global health is a critical area of international cooperation and diplomacy. The COVID19 pandemic highlighted the importance of global health systems and the need for coordinated responses to health crises. Nations work together to address health challenges, promote public health, and ensure access to medical care for all.

The World Health Organization (WHO) plays a central role in global health diplomacy. The WHO coordinates international efforts to monitor and respond to health threats, provides guidance and support to member states, and promotes health equity. Through the International Health Regulations, countries commit to reporting health emergencies and cooperating on responses.

Pandemics and infectious diseases pose significant threats to global health. International cooperation is essential for monitoring outbreaks, developing vaccines and treatments, and implementing public health measures. The global response to the COVID19 pandemic involved unprecedented collaboration on research, vaccine distribution, and public health strategies.

Health diplomacy extends beyond pandemics to address a wide range of health issues. Nations work together to combat diseases like HIV/AIDS, tuberculosis, and malaria, promote maternal and child health, and address noncommunicable diseases like cancer and diabetes. Health diplomacy also involves efforts to strengthen health systems, improve access to healthcare, and address social determinants of health.

Humanitarian health aid is an important component of global health diplomacy. Nations provide medical assistance to communities affected by conflicts, natural disasters, and other crises. Humanitarian health aid includes emergency medical care, vaccination campaigns, and support for healthcare infrastructure.

Global health diplomacy faces numerous challenges. Health inequities, resource limitations, and political factors can hinder progress. However, the importance of global health makes cooperation essential. Through health diplomacy, nations can work together to protect public health and build resilient health systems.

## 11

## Chapter 11: The Influence of Media and Information

Media and information play a powerful role in shaping international relations and public opinion. The flow of information can influence perceptions, shape narratives, and drive political and social change. Nations use media and information as tools of statecraft to promote their interests and values.

International media networks like CNN, BBC, and Al Jazeera have a global reach and can shape public opinion on international issues. These networks provide news and analysis, influencing how people understand and interpret events around the world. Nations may use international media to communicate their policies, respond to crises, and promote their image.

Social media has transformed the landscape of information and communication. Platforms like Twitter, Facebook, and Instagram allow for realtime communication and engagement with global audiences. Nations use social media to connect with people around the world, share information, and build soft power. Social media also provides a platform for citizen journalism and grassroots movements.

Disinformation and propaganda are significant challenges in the information age. Nations and nonstate actors may spread false information to manipulate public opinion, sow discord, and achieve strategic goals. Combating disinformation requires coordinated efforts, media literacy, and transparency.

Information diplomacy is the strategic use of information to influence international relations. Nations may engage in public diplomacy campaigns, cultural exchanges, and media outreach to shape perceptions and build goodwill. Information diplomacy also involves efforts to promote freedom of the press, protect journalists, and ensure access to accurate and reliable information.

The role of media and information in international relations is complex and multifaceted. While media can promote understanding and cooperation, it can also be a tool of manipulation and conflict. Navigating the challenges and opportunities of the information age is a critical task for modern statecraft.

# 12

# Chapter 12: The Interplay of Nationalism and Globalism

Nationalism and globalism are two powerful forces that shape the dynamics of international relations. Nationalism emphasizes the interests and identity of individual nations, promoting sovereignty, selfdetermination, and cultural pride. Globalism, on the other hand, advocates for interconnectedness, cooperation, and the integration of economies and societies.

Nationalism can be a source of unity and strength. It fosters a sense of belonging and loyalty to the nationstate. Nationalist movements have played a crucial role in the struggle for independence and selfdetermination, leading to the formation of new states and the redrawing of borders. However, nationalism can also lead to exclusion, xenophobia, and conflict. Extreme forms of nationalism can undermine international cooperation and fuel tensions between nations.

Globalism promotes the idea that nations are interconnected and interdependent. It emphasizes the benefits of cooperation and integration in addressing global challenges like trade, climate change, and security. The rise of global institutions, multinational corporations, and transnational networks has accelerated the process of globalization. Globalism advocates for open borders, free trade, and the free flow of information and people.

The interplay between nationalism and globalism creates a dynamic and complex international landscape. Nations must navigate the tension between maintaining their sovereignty and embracing global cooperation. This balance is crucial for addressing global challenges and promoting peace and prosperity.

# 13

# Chapter 13: The Influence of Religion and Ideology

Religion and ideology are powerful forces that shape the identities and policies of nations. They provide a framework for understanding the world, guiding political decisions, and influencing international relations. Religion and ideology can be sources of unity and conflict, cooperation and division.

Religion has played a central role in the history of many nations. It shapes cultural identities, social norms, and moral values. Religious institutions and leaders often wield significant influence over political decisions. Religious diplomacy involves engaging with religious communities and leaders to promote peace, tolerance, and mutual understanding.

Ideologies, such as democracy, communism, and capitalism, provide a blueprint for governance and economic organization. They influence the policies and strategies of nations, shaping their interactions with other states. Ideological conflicts have been a driving force behind many historical and contemporary geopolitical struggles.

The influence of religion and ideology on international relations is complex.

They can promote peace and cooperation or fuel conflict and division. Understanding the role of religion and ideology is essential for navigating the challenges and opportunities of the global stage.

# 14

# Chapter 14: The Role of NonState Actors

Nonstate actors play an increasingly important role in international relations. These actors, which include multinational corporations, nongovernmental organizations (NGOs), and transnational advocacy networks, can influence policies, shape public opinion, and address global challenges.

Multinational corporations have significant economic power and can influence trade, investment, and development. They operate across borders, creating jobs, driving innovation, and contributing to economic growth. However, they can also contribute to inequality, environmental degradation, and exploitation.

NGOs and transnational advocacy networks work to address social, environmental, and humanitarian issues. They provide aid, conduct research, and advocate for policy changes. These organizations can mobilize public support, influence governments, and shape international agendas.

The rise of nonstate actors has transformed the landscape of international relations. They provide new opportunities for cooperation and innovation, but also present challenges for traditional statecentric approaches to diplomacy and governance.

# 15

# Chapter 15: The Dynamics of Regionalism

Regionalism refers to the process by which countries within a specific region form alliances and cooperate on various issues. Regional organizations and agreements play a crucial role in promoting economic integration, political stability, and security within regions.

The European Union (EU) is one of the most successful examples of regional integration. The EU promotes economic cooperation, political integration, and social cohesion among its member states. It has created a single market, established a common currency (the euro), and developed common policies on various issues.

Other regions have also pursued regional integration. The African Union (AU) aims to promote unity, peace, and development across Africa. The Association of Southeast Asian Nations (ASEAN) focuses on economic cooperation, security, and cultural exchange in Southeast Asia. The Organization of American States (OAS) promotes democracy, human rights, and development in the Americas.

Regionalism provides a platform for addressing regional challenges and promoting common interests. However, it can also create tensions and rivalries between regions. Understanding the dynamics of regionalism is

## CHAPTER 15: THE DYNAMICS OF REGIONALISM

essential for navigating the complexities of international relations.

# 16

# Chapter 16: The Impact of Migration and Diasporas

Migration and diasporas have a profound impact on international relations. The movement of people across borders shapes economies, cultures, and societies. Diasporas, or communities of people living outside their country of origin, can influence the politics and policies of both their host and home countries.

Migration can be driven by various factors, including economic opportunities, conflicts, environmental changes, and social networks. Migrants contribute to the economic growth and cultural diversity of their host countries. However, migration can also create challenges, such as social integration, labor market competition, and political tensions.

Diasporas can act as bridges between their host and home countries. They contribute to economic development through remittances, investments, and entrepreneurship. Diasporas also promote cultural exchange, fostering mutual understanding and cooperation. However, they can also be a source of tension and conflict, particularly if they are involved in political or ethnic disputes.

# CHAPTER 16: THE IMPACT OF MIGRATION AND DIASPORAS

Migration and diasporas are dynamic and multifaceted phenomena. Understanding their impact on international relations is essential for addressing the opportunities and challenges they present.

# 17

# Chapter 17: The Role of Intelligence and Espionage

Intelligence and espionage are critical components of statecraft. They provide valuable information and insights that shape national security, foreign policy, and international relations. Intelligence agencies collect, analyze, and disseminate information to support decisionmaking and protect national interests.

Espionage involves the covert collection of information, often through clandestine operations and human intelligence (HUMINT). Intelligence agencies use various methods, including surveillance, cyber espionage, and undercover operations, to gather information about potential threats and adversaries.

Intelligence agencies also engage in counterintelligence efforts to protect against espionage and sabotage by foreign actors. These efforts involve identifying and neutralizing threats, such as spies, hackers, and terrorists.

The role of intelligence and espionage in international relations is complex and often controversial. While they are essential for national security, their activities can also raise ethical and legal concerns. Balancing the need for

## CHAPTER 17: THE ROLE OF INTELLIGENCE AND ESPIONAGE

intelligence with respect for privacy and human rights is a critical challenge for modern statecraft.

# 18

# Chapter 18: The Influence of Global Finance

Global finance is a powerful force that shapes the dynamics of international relations. Financial markets, institutions, and flows of capital have a profound impact on economies, policies, and geopolitical stability. Nations use financial tools to promote economic growth, manage risks, and exert influence on the global stage.

Financial institutions, such as central banks, investment banks, and sovereign wealth funds, play a crucial role in global finance. Central banks regulate monetary policy, stabilize currencies, and manage inflation. Investment banks facilitate international trade and investment, providing capital and financial services. Sovereign wealth funds invest in a diverse range of assets, promoting economic stability and growth.

International financial organizations, such as the International Monetary Fund (IMF) and the World Bank, provide financial support and policy advice to countries facing economic challenges. These organizations play a key role in promoting global financial stability and development.

Financial markets, including stock exchanges, bond markets, and foreign

## CHAPTER 18: THE INFLUENCE OF GLOBAL FINANCE

exchange markets, enable the flow of capital across borders. These markets are influenced by various factors, including economic indicators, political events, and investor sentiment.

The influence of global finance on international relations is complex and multifaceted. Financial crises, currency fluctuations, and capital flows can create opportunities and challenges for nations. Understanding the dynamics of global finance is essential for navigating the interconnected world economy.

# 19

# Chapter 19: The Ethics of Sovereign Influence

The exercise of sovereign influence raises important ethical questions. Nations must navigate the balance between pursuing their interests and upholding moral principles. Ethical considerations are essential for building trust, legitimacy, and cooperation in international relations.

The use of power, whether military, economic, or diplomatic, must be guided by ethical principles. Nations must consider the impact of their actions on human rights, justice, and the wellbeing of people. Ethical statecraft involves promoting peace, protecting the vulnerable, and addressing global challenges.

Transparency and accountability are key components of ethical statecraft. Nations must be open about their actions and decisions, providing clear justifications and being accountable for their consequences. This transparency builds trust and credibility in the international community.

The promotion of human rights and social justice is a fundamental ethical imperative. Nations must work to address inequality, discrimination, and injustice, both within their borders and globally. This commitment to human rights enhances moral leadership and influence.

# CHAPTER 19: THE ETHICS OF SOVEREIGN INFLUENCE

Ethical dilemmas often arise in international relations. Balancing national interests with global responsibilities, addressing conflicts between moral principles, and navigating complex ethical issues require careful consideration and judgment. Ethical statecraft is an ongoing and evolving process.

# 20

# Chapter 20: The Role of Science and Innovation in Global Challenges

Science and innovation play a crucial role in addressing global challenges and shaping the future of international relations. Advances in science and technology can drive economic growth, improve quality of life, and provide solutions to pressing issues like climate change, public health, and food security.

Scientific research and innovation are essential for economic development and competitiveness. Nations that invest in research and development (R&D) can lead in cuttingedge fields like artificial intelligence, biotechnology, and renewable energy. These advancements create new industries, jobs, and economic opportunities.

International collaboration in science and innovation fosters mutual understanding and cooperation. Joint research projects, scientific exchange programs, and global initiatives promote the sharing of knowledge and resources. This collaboration enhances the capacity to address global challenges and promotes scientific progress.

www.ingramcontent.com/pod-product-compliance
Lightning Source LLC
LaVergne TN
LVHW020456080526
838202LV00057B/5980